Primordial Strength Systems Underground Alpha Z Original Beast Training

By Steven Helmicki

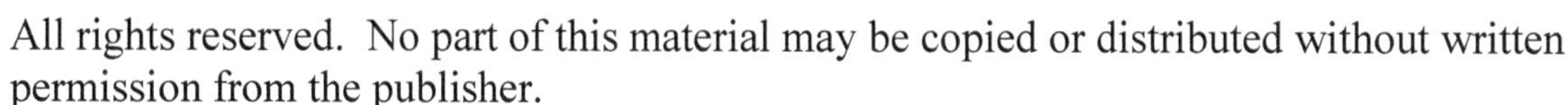

ISBN: 978-0-557-29267-7

These workouts are to be performed one after the other in the order that they appear. A three day per week training schedule is the best format, however take the necessary time to recover so full output can be given.

Train to Win. Period.

Workout 1

Kettlebell swings 12kg x 2 immediately followed by 24kg x 2 immediately followed by 48kg x 2 repeat 3 times non-stop

Hydration

4kg kettlebell pullovers x 8

Sumo kettlebell deadlifts 12kg x 2 immediately followed by 24kg x 2 immediately followed by 48kg x 2 repeat 3 times non-stop

Hydration

4kg kettlebell pllovers x 8

Kettlebell front squats 12kg x 2 immediately followed by 24kg x 2 immediately followed by 48kg x 2 repeat 3 times non-stop

Hydration

4kg kettlebell pullovers x 8

Single kettlebell cleans 12kg x 1 immediately followed by 24kg x 1 immediately followed by 48 kg x 1 repeat 3 times non-stop

Hydration

4kg kettlebell pullovers x 8

Kettlebell curls 4kg x 2 immediately followed by 8kg x 2 immediately followed by 12kg x 2 immediately followed by 24kg x 2 repeat 3 times non-stop

4kg kettlebell pullovers x 8

Hydration

Bodyweight broad jump x 1 immediately followed by 10 yard sprint repeat 5 times non-stop

Stretch

Workout 2

150 lb tire flip x1 immediately followed by 300 lb tire flip x 1 immediately followed by 450lb tire flip x 1 repeat 2 times

4kg kettlebell pullovers x 3 immediately followed by 8kg kettlebell pullovers x 3

Hydration

185 lb box squat x 2 immediately followed by 370lb box squat x 2 repeat 3 times

4 kg kettlebell pullovers x 3 immediately followed by 8kg kettlebell pullovers x 3

Hydration

Standing press 95lbs x 3 immediately followed by 190lbs x 3 repeat 2 times

4kg kettlebell pullovers x 3 immediately followed by 8kg kettlebell pullovers x 3

Hydration

Straight bar curls 70lbs x 3 immediately followed by 140lbs x 3 repeat 2 times non-stop

4kg kettlebell pullovers x 3 immediately followed by 8kg kettlebell pullovers x 3

Hydration

Landmine twist with 35lbs x 3 immediately followed by landmine twist with 70lbs x 3
Repeat 3 times

Dynamic knee ups x 6 per leg

Broad jump and 5 yard dash

Broad jump and 10 yard dash

Broad jump and 20 yard dash

Workout 3

Trap bar deadlift 250lbs x 2 immediately followed by 500lbs x 2 repeat 4 times

Hydration

Kettlebell bench 24kg x 4 immediately followed by 48kg x 4 repeat 4 times

Hydration

Bent over rows 185lbs x 1 immediately followed by 370lbs x 1 repeat 3 times

Hydration

Chins with 45lbs x 2 immediately followed by 90lbs x 2 repeat 3 times

Hydration

Triceps pushdowns 100 lbs x 2 immediately followed by 200lbs x 2 repeat 4 times

Hydration

Neck harness 24kg kettlebell extension/flexion x 75 reps

Kettlebell swings 48kg x 20 reps

Average band broad jump immediately followed by first two step sprint with average band repeat 6 times

Workout 4-Monster Flush

Empty bar squats 150 reps in as short a time as possible

Empty bar bench 150 reps in as short a time as possible

Manta ray Hise shrugs 135lbs x 150 reps in as short a time as possible

Empty bar curls 150 reps in as short a time as possible

Workout 5

Sandbag cleans 50 lbs x 1 immediately followed by 100lbs x 1 immediately followed by 150lbs x 1 repeat 3 times non-stop

Hydration

12 inch box jumps 4kg x 2 immediately followed by 8kg x 2 immediately followed by 16kg x 2 repeat 3 times no-stop

Hydration

Nautilus Pullover 100 lbs x 3 immediately followed by 200lbs x 3 repeat 3 times non-stop

Hydration

Average band curls to face x 4 immediately followed by strong band x 4 repeat 3 times non-stop

Hydration

Close grip bench 185lbs x 2 immediately followed by 365lbs x 2 repeat 2 times

Hydration

Bosu neck head stands bodyweight x 8 immediately followed by 20lb vest x 8 repeat three times

Hydration

Ten yard dash x 1 immediately followed by 10 yard dash with vest x 1 repeat 4 times non-stop

Workout 6

Yoke walk 135lbs x 20 yards immediately followed by 270lbs x 20 yards repeat 2 times non-stop

Hydration

Kettlebell broad jumps 4kg x 1 immediately followed by 8kg x 1 imediately followed by 12 kg x 1 repeat 3 times non stop

Hydration

Pull-ups bodyweight x 2 immediately followed by 40 lbs x 2 immediately followed by 80lbs x 2 repeat 2 times non-stop

Hydration

Straight bar shrugs 250lbs x 5 immediately followed by 500lbs x 5 repeat 2 times non-stop

Hydration

Kettlebell curls 8kg x 75 reps

Hydration

Kettlebell swings 32kg x 1 immediately followed by 48kg x 1 repeat 3 times

Hydration

75 yard dash x 1
Walk back rest
15 yard dash x 3

Workout 7

Husafell replica 100 lbs x 1 immediately followed by 200lbs x 1 repeat 3 times non-stop

Hydration

Kettlebell presses 24kg x 1 immediately followed by 48kg x 1 repeat 2 times non-stop

Hydration

Kettlebell shrugs 24kg x 10 immediately followed by 48kg x 10 repeat 2 times non-stop

Hydration

Dips bodyweight x 2 immediately followed by 50lbs x 2 immediately followed by 100lbs x 2 repeat 3 times non-stop

Hydration

12kg kettlebell curls x 40 reps

Hydration

Nautilus 4 way neck 3 plates x 3 immediately followed by 6 plates x 3 repeat 3 times non-stop all positions

30 yard dash x 2 walkback rest

Workout 8

Pin squat 12 inch movement 350lbs x 1 immediately followed by 700lbs x 1 repeat 3 times non-stop

Hydration

Sled rows 6 plates x 3 immediately followed by 12 plates x 3 repeat 3 times non-stop

Hydration

Vertical jumps bodyweight x 2 immediately followed by 12kg kettlebell verticals x 2 repeat 3 times non-stop

Hydration

Sled curls 4 plates x 2 immediately followed by 8 plates x 2 repeat 3 times non-stop

Hydration

Kettlebell high pulls 24 kg x 1 immediately followed by 48 kg x 1 repeat 3 times non-stop

Workout 9- kettlebell flush

8kg front squats x 50 reps

8kg bench x 50 reps

8kg bent rows x 50 reps

8kg curls x 50 reps

Neck harness with 8kg kettlebell x 50 reps

Workout 10

Kettlebell farmers walk 24kg x 15 yards immediately followed by 48kg x 15 yards repeat 3 times non-stop

Hydration

Pin deadlifts from the knees 300lbs x 1 immediately followed by 600lbs x 1 repeat 3 times non-stop

Hydration

Average reverse band bench 225lbs x 1 immediately followed by 450lbs x 1 repeat 2 times non-stop

Hydration

Dumbbell hammer curls 45lbs x 3 immediately followed by 90 lbs x 3 repeat 3 times non-stop

Hydration

Landmine combat handle side bends 70lbs x 2 immediately followed by 140lbs x 2 repeat 2 times non-stop

Hydration

100 yard sprint

Workout 11

Power cleans 135 lbs x1 immediately followed by 270 lbs x 1 repeat three times non-stop

Hydration

Bench press 135lbs x 3 immediately followed by 270lbs x 3 repeat 3 times non-stop

Hydration

Hise shrugs 250lbs x 5 immediately followed by 500lbs x 3 repeat 3 times non-stop

Hydration

5 yard dash x 2

30 yard dash x 1

10 yard dash x 2

40 yard dash x 1

Workout 12

Full squat 250 lbs x 1 immediately followed by 500lbs x 1 repeat 3 times non-stop

Hydration

Deadlift 250lbs x 1 immediately followed by 500lbs x 1 repeat 3 times non-stop

Hydration

Bench press 150 lbs x 1 immediately followed by 300lbs x 1 repeat 3 times non-stop

Hydration

Straight bar curls 65lbs x 3 immediately followed by 135lbs x 3 repeat 3 times non-stop

Hydration

Kettlebell swings 16kg x 2 immediately followed by 32kg x 2 repeat 3 times non-stop

Hydration

Neck harness extension/flexion 12kg x 3 immediately followed by 24kg x 3 repeat 3 times non-stop

Workout 13

Round stone load 100 lbs x 1 immediately followed by 200lbs x 1 immediately followed by 300 lbs x 1 repeat 2 times non-stop

Hydration

Dumbbell bent rows 75lbs x 3 immediately followed by 150lbs x 3 repeat 3 times non-stop

Hydration

High pulls 90lbs x 3 immediately followed by 180lbs x 3 repeat 3 times non-stop

Hydration

Chins 20 reps

Dips 20 reps

Nautilus neck 30 reps all four ways

Hydration

4 x 20 yard dashes walkback rest

Workout 14

Seated good mornings 160lbs x 2 immediately followed by 320lbs x 2 repeat 3 times non-stop

Hydration

Band broad jumps light x 2 immediately followed by average x 2 immediately followed by strong x 2 repeat 3 times non-stop

Hydration

Straight bar curls 45 lbs x 5 immediately followed by 90lbs x 3 repeat 3 times non-stop

Hydration

3 x 60 yard sprints walk back rest

Workout 15

Pool sprints bodyweight x 10 yards immediately followed by 20lb vest x 10 yards repeat 7 times non-stop

Workout 16

Bicycle sprints 35 yards bodyweight immediately followed by 35 yards plus 50 lb weight vest repeat 4 times non-stop

Workout 17

10 yard sprint bodyweight immediately followed by 10 yard sprint with 20lb vest repeat 8 times non-stop

Workout 18

Empty bar squat 200 reps in as short a period as possible

Empty bar front press 200 reps in as short a period as possible

Empty bar rows 200 reps in as short a period as possible

Monster mini-band curls x 200 reps in as short a period as possible

Workout 19

Squat 135 lbs x 1 immediately followed by 270lbs x 1 immediately followed by 405 lbs x 1 repeat 3 times non-stop

Hydration

Bench press 100 lbs x 2 immediately followed by 200lbs x 2 immediately followed by 300lbs x 2 repeat 2 times non-stop

Hydration

Bent rows 100lbs x 2 immediately followed by 200lbs x 2 immediately followed by 300 lbs x 2 repeat 2 times non-stop

Hydration

Chins 50lbs x 1 immediately followed by 100lbs x 1 repeat 2 times non-stop

Hydration

Dips 50lbs x 1 immediately followed by 100lbs x 1 repeat 2 times non-stop

Hydration

Neck harness extension/flexion 24kg x 1 immediately followed by 48kg x 1 repeat 3 times

Workout 20

Barbell snatch 75lbs x 1 immediately followed by 150lbs x 1 repeat 4 times non-stop

Hydration

Front squat 135 lbs x 1 immediately followed by 270lbs x 1 repeat 3 times non-stop

Hydration

Nautilus pullovers 70 x 4 immediately followed by 140lbs x 4 repeat 3 times non-stop

Hydration

Nautilus supinated grip pulldowns 100lbs x 2 immediately followed by 200 lbs x 2 repeat 3 times non-stop

Hydration

Nautilus 4 way neck 100 reps per side

Hydration

200 yard sprint

Workout 21

300lb tire flip 5 flips downhill immediately followed by 5 flips uphill

Hydration

Kettlebell swings 12kg x 6 immediately followed by 24kg x 6 immediately followed by 48kg x 6 repeat 2 times non-stop

Hydration

4 x 25 yard dash walk back rest

S	W	O	T

S	W	O	T

S	W	O	T

S	W	O	T

S	W	O	T

S	W	O	T

S W O T

www.ingramcontent.com/pod-product-compliance
Ingram Content Group UK Ltd.
Pitfield, Milton Keynes, MK11 3LW, UK
UKHW051133260726
13967UKWH00010B/3022

9 780557 292677